D1442261

# FOOTBALL
## TIME!

by Brendan Flynn

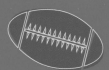

BUMBA BOoKS™

LERNER PUBLICATIONS ◆ MINNEAPOLIS

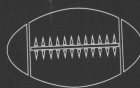

**Note to Educators:**

Throughout this book, you'll find critical thinking questions. These can be used to engage young readers in thinking critically about the topic and in using the text and photos to do so.

Lerner Publications Company
A division of Lerner Publishing Group, Inc.
241 First Avenue North
Minneapolis, MN 55401 USA

For reading levels and more information, look up this title at www.lernerbooks.com.

**Library of Congress Cataloging-in-Publication Data**

Names: Flynn, Brendan, 1977–
Title: Football time! / by Brendan Flynn.
Description: Minneapolis : Lerner Publications, [2017] | Series: Bumba Books — Sports Time! | Includes bibliographical references and index.
Identifiers: LCCN 2016001059 (print) | LCCN 2016005880 (ebook) | ISBN 9781512414332 (lb : alk. paper) | ISBN 9781512415414 (pb : alk. paper) | ISBN 9781512415421 (eb pdf)
Subjects: LCSH: Football—United States—Juvenile literature.
Classification: LCC GV950.7 .F59 2017 (print) | LCC GV950.7 (ebook) | DDC 796.332—dc23

LC record available at http://lccn.loc.gov/2016001059

Manufactured in the United States of America
1 – VP – 7/15/16

Expand learning beyond the printed book. Download free, complementary educational resources for this book from our website, www.lernerresource.com.

# Table of Contents

# We Play Football

Football is a sport.

People play it in fall.

pads

ball

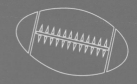

helmet

You need a ball.

You need a helmet.

You also need pads.

They protect your body.

**Why do football players protect their bodies?**

Football fields are on grass.

They have white lines.

The lines mark the end zones and sidelines.

**Why do you think the end zones are a different color?**

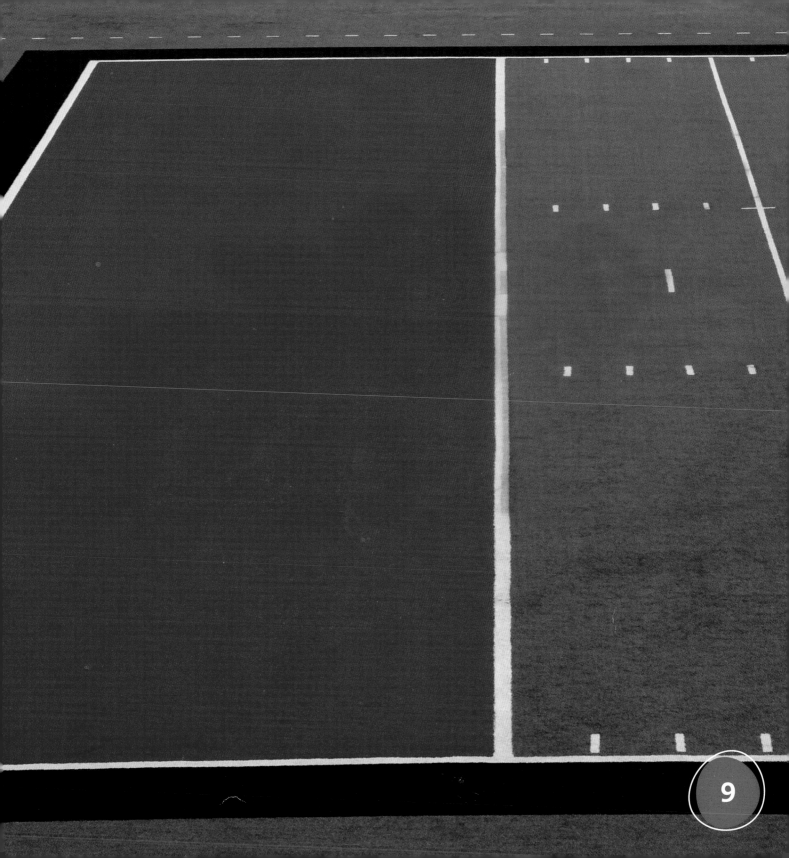

Football games have two teams.

The game is starting.

One team kicks the ball.

Players run with the ball.

They can pass it to a teammate.

The other team tries to stop them.

They tackle the player with

the ball.

13

A player carries the ball into the

end zone.

That is a touchdown.

It is worth 6 points.

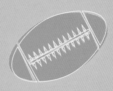

Now the other team gets
the ball.
The team with the most
points at the end of the
game wins.

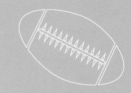

You can watch football at a stadium.

Many games are on TV too.

**Where else might you see a football game?**

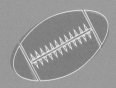

Playing football is fun.

It is a great way to spend

an afternoon.

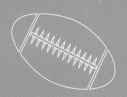

# Football Field

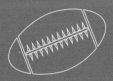

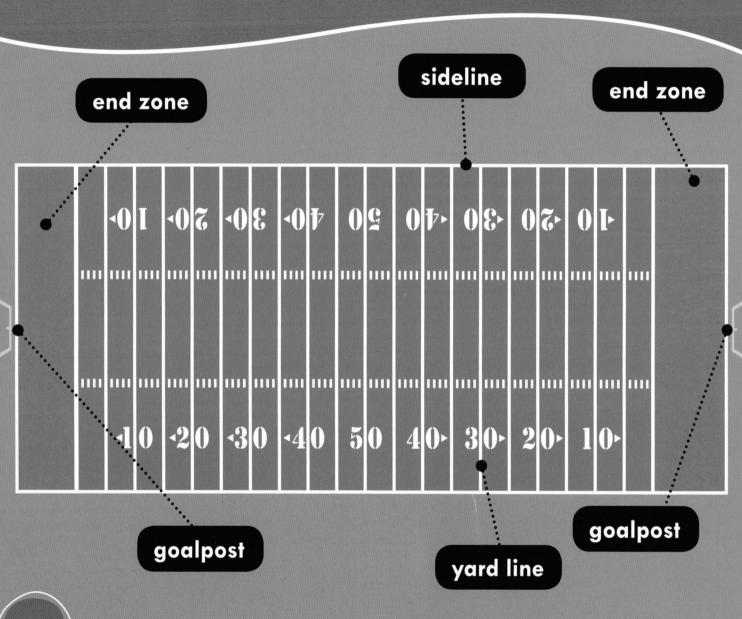

end zone

sideline

end zone

goalpost

yard line

goalpost

# Picture Glossary

**end zones**

the areas at the ends of a football field

**pads**

soft things players wear to protect their bodies in a game

**stadium**

a large building where people can watch a game

**tackle**

to bring another player to the ground

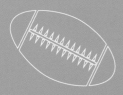

# Index

# Read More

Mattern, Joanne. *I Know Football.* Ann Arbor, MI: Cherry Lake Publishing, 2013.

Morey, Allan. *Football.* Minneapolis: Bullfrog Books, 2015.

Nelson, Robin. *Football Is Fun!* Minneapolis: Lerner Publications, 2014.

## Photo Credits

The images in this book are used with the permission of: © Andrew Rich/iStock.com, p. 5; © Brocreative/Shutterstock.com, pp. 6–7, 10, 23 (top right); © SAJE/Shutterstock.com, pp. 8–9, 23 (top left); © Amy Myers/Shutterstock.com, pp. 13, 23 (bottom right); © wacomme/iStock.com, p. 14; © bikeriderlondon/Shutterstock.com, pp. 16–17; © ActionPics/iStock.com, p. 18; © monkeybusinessimages/iStock.com, p. 21; © Willierossin/Shutterstock.com, p. 22; © Adam Derewecki/Shutterstock.com, p. 23 (bottom left). Front Cover: © Rob Hainer/Shutterstock.com.